Bright Eyed®

First edition published in 2022
By Everything Slight Pepper.
P.O. Box 1373 St. Vincent Street
Port of Spain, Trinidad and Tobago.

ISBN: 978-976-95350-5-3

Written by **Jeunanne Alkins & Neala Bhagwansingh**

Illustrated by **Sayada Ramdial**

Layout, Graphics & Typesetting by **Jeunanne Alkins**

Research by **Joshua Lue Chee Kong**

The Magnificent Seven are heritage sites located on the western side of the Queen's Park Savannah in Trinidad and Tobago. While the mansions - Queen's Royal College, Hayes Court, Mille Fleurs, Roomor (Ambard's House), Whitehall (Rosenweg), Archbishop's Palace and Stollmeyer's Castle (Killarney) are real, THE MOST MAGNIFICENT is how we imagine they would tell their own story.

www.wearebrighteyed.com **@wearebrighteyed**

For my biggest supporter, my gran Joycey, who loved telling stories about the past and amazed us with her ability to recall every little detail.

- JEUNANNE

Mrs. Mille Fleurs sneezed away cobwebs from her sleepy shutters. A kite woke her up as it sailed back and forth, tickling her grey, aging balcony. She thought she heard children talking.

hhhChoO

Ah yes, she glimpsed them, across the street on the Queen's Park Savannah.
A little boy whispered to the others, **"I wonder if they are even alive?"**
"Mayyyybeeeee," one of the boys shrugged, **"Maybe they are taking a nap!"**

The little girl screamed out,
"EXCUSE ME, ARE YOU ASLEEP?"

Mrs. Mille Fleurs stirred gently,
trying to hide that she had dozed off.

NO, NO
I WAS UHHMM
JUST RESTING MY SHUTTERS

She raised her roof trying to get the
attention of the other houses on the street.

Professor QRC, a stern gentleman at the end, was grumbling, trying to restart the stopped clock in his tower.

Next door, Lady Hayes Court was trying to shake off dried leaves that had piled onto her roof.

Through the trees she could hear Dr. Roomor, who was fast asleep, rattling her heavy iron balcony with noisy, rusty snores.

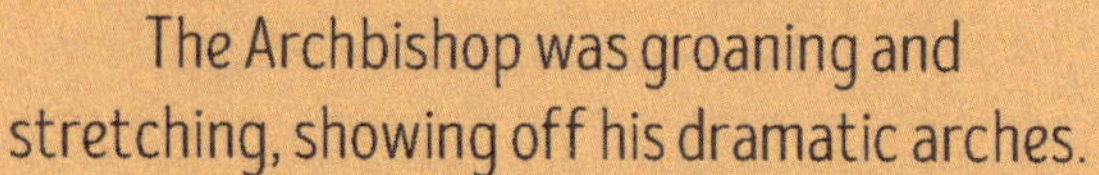

The Archbishop was groaning and stretching, showing off his dramatic arches.

Over the fence, Minister Whitehall was trying to keep her windows closed, as a gust of breeze blew through her coral corridors.

On the furthest end, Sir Stollmeyer was making a commotion, trying to find where he had put the keys to his front door.

The boy shrugged, **"See, I told you! My daddy said these old buildings no longer have stories to tell!"** The girl interrupted, **"Well, my mummy said that they are an important part of our history! I'm just not too sure what that means,"** she added thoughtfully.

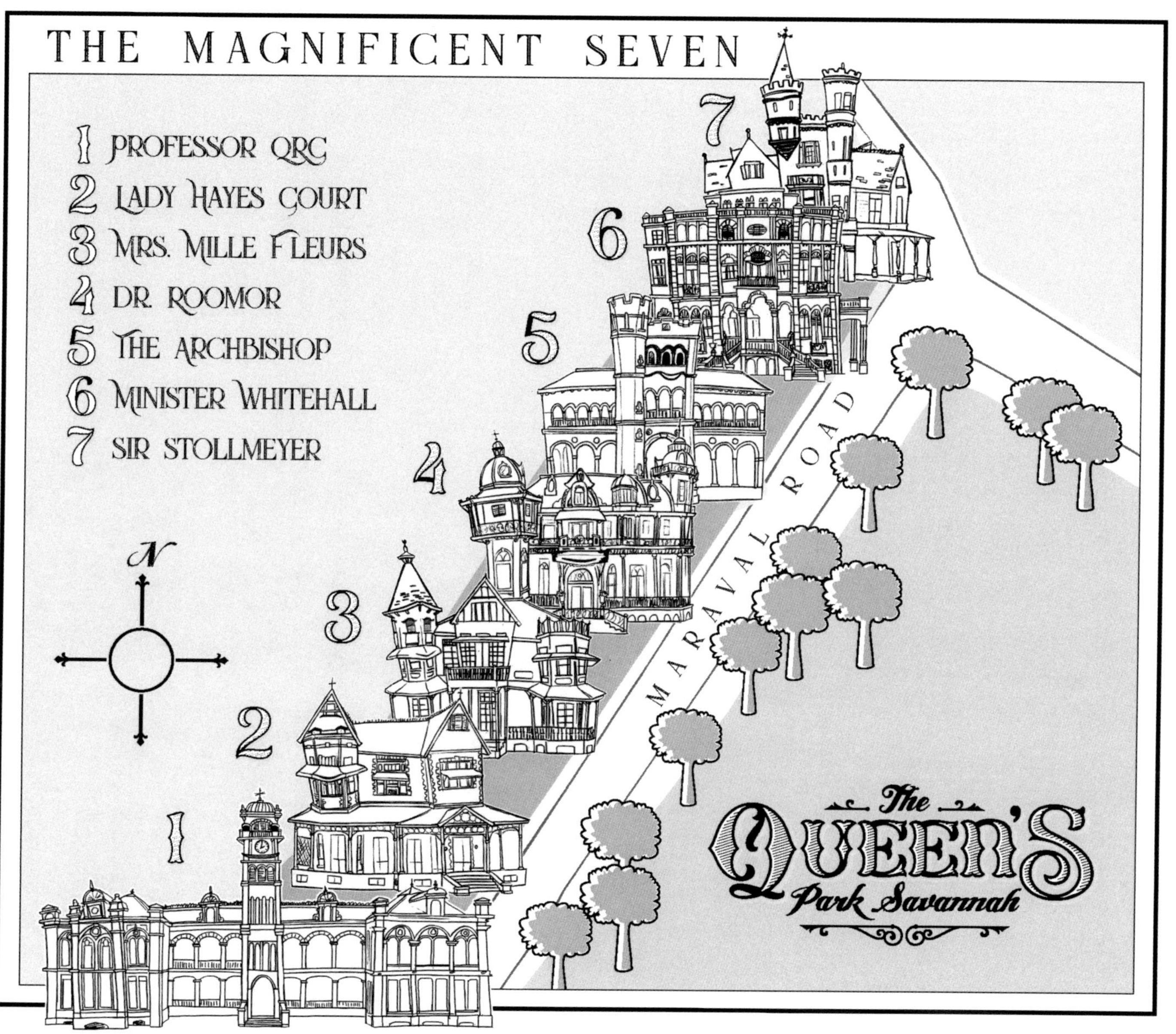

"Sorry children, the hearing is not as good as it used to be," Mrs. Mille Fleurs apologised. "First you must understand that we are known as the Magnificent Seven and yes, we've been around for over a hundred years!"

"Trinidad and Tobago was really different back then, there were few motorcars. We had tramcars instead, and people could ride them all the way around the Savannah and it only cost two cents! Visitors came from all over the country to take a ride while the Police Band played songs in front of Minister Whitehall," she explained.

The others finally perked up, creaking and groaning a little, shaking off their dusty walls. Feeling really pleased with herself, Mrs. Mille Fleurs spun the statue on her fountain. **"I was a gift from a wife to her husband. There were many social gatherings in my gardens and in my grand rooms. Important people brought joy to everyone outside and inside my walls."**

The children listened intently. Mrs. Mille Fleurs continued

"And naturally, as the most magnificent, I..."

"I beg your pardon!"
Dr. Roomor objected.
The other houses glared at her.
"YOU?
What makes you think that you are
THE
MOST MAGNIFICENT?"

Silence filled the street.

Everyone looked at Mrs. Mille Fleurs, waiting for her answer.

The proud lady paused for a moment.
“Well, I definitely think the oldest is the most magnificent...”

Lady Hayes Court huffed her hedges
“Well, I was built in 1908!”

Mrs. Mille Fleurs smiled proudly
“As I was saying, I was built way back in 1904!”

Minister Whitehall and Dr. Roomor interrupted loudly.
“WE WERE BUILT IN 1904!”

“Err hmm, 1903, here,” called out the Archbishop.

Professor QRC chimed his bell to demand attention. **“You are all certainly not the oldest. I was built in 1902.”**

Sir Stollmeyer shouted... **“If age makes a difference, then you need to know I’m older than the professor. Even though I was finished in 1904, they began building me in 1902 as well!”**

1904

MRS. MILLE FLEURS

MINISTER WHITEHALL

DR. ROOMOR

CITY OF PORT OF SPA
ARCHIVES
OFFICIAL RECO

1903

THE ARCHBISHOP

1902

PROFESSOR QRC

SIR STOLLMEYER

One of the boys asked, **“So is it your age that makes you the most magnificent?”**

"I don't think that's quite right." Mrs. Mille Fleurs suddenly felt embarrassed, realising that she was not the oldest. **“Age probably has less to do with it,”** she whispered.

Sir Stollmeyer interrupted, gathering his solid structure.
“I dare say...

"...Surely impressive structure has something to do with it! Look at my elaborate form," he gave a stony salute, "I am modelled after a real castle in Scotland!"

Mrs. Mille Fleurs gazed at her own cast iron brackets shining against her pale walls,
"I have decorative designs too! Have you seen my delicate railings? My name means a thousand flowers, how much more beautifully magnificent is that?"

“Well, if it is about impressive structure, then I should be considered the only choice,” Dr. Roomor rattled her decorative wrought iron. **“They call me the cast iron mansion. Look at my railings, gates, stairs, balconies, towers, windows and roof. I am decorated all fancy, just like a movie star!”**

Lady Hayes Court examined her ordinary, sturdy build. She added softly,
"Well, I quite like my neat, simple lines. There is merit in modesty."

Minister Whitehall raised a thoughtful voice.
"I think she's right. Simplicity is beautiful. Look at me with my one colour and my stunning white coral walls."

The Archbishop coughed his displeasure.

"How can you say simple is better than my grand colourful arches and tall tower?"

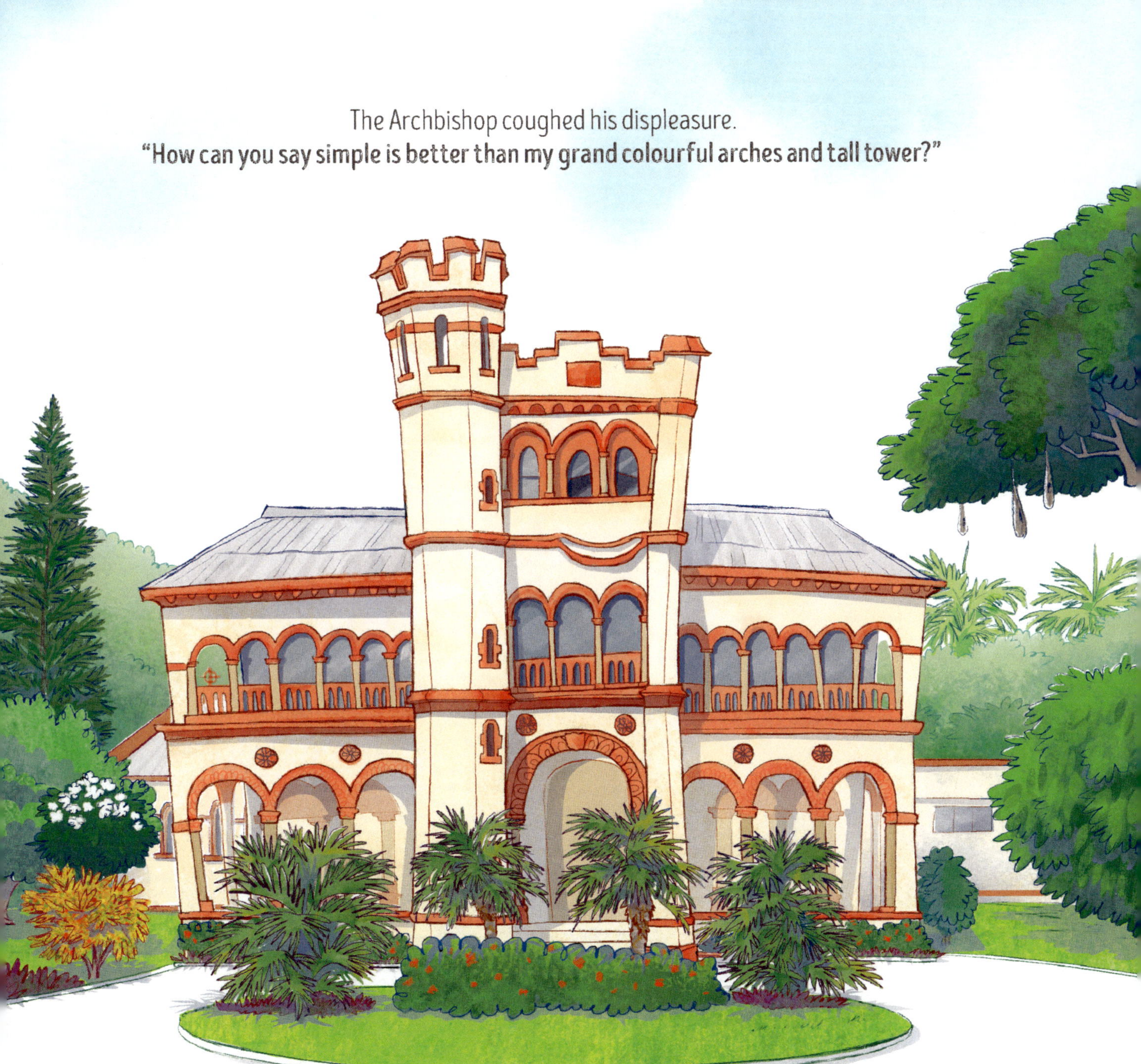

"To be accurate," Professor QRC corrected,
"I also have an impressive tower, **and it even has a clock!"**

Confused, the boy asked.
"So is it how you look that makes you the most magnificent?"

Mrs. Mille Fleurs was now worried that they might be teaching the children improper values. Before she could help straighten out the mess, Dr. Roomor cleared her columns.

The Golden Age of Cinema

“Well, I believe it’s the people who live in us that make us magnificent. Important families have always lived in me. One even built the first movie theatres in our country,” she said.

Mrs. Mille Fleurs whistled, "**My people built important buildings too. One of my families built the largest general store in the city of Port of Spain at the time. It was three storeys high and had fifteen different departments!**"

"**Wow!**" The girl said excitedly, "**That is important! So, is it the families that lived in you that makes you the most magnificent?**"

Lady Hayes Court chimed in,
"I was named after Bishop Thomas Hayes and I've been home to the Anglican bishops since I was built. They were responsible for building schools and churches and have helped many people all over the country!"

The Archbishop scrunched his arches.
"Yes, I believe being a home to charitable people who help the community matters too! I kept Father Bouche safe in my tower when he had leprosy. He built two schools and a church in St. James and translated the catechism manual from English to Chinese and Hindi!"

"Soooooo,"
the boy whispered,
"Is charity work something that makes you the most magnificent?"

Sir Stollmeyer tipped his roof. "This argument does not hold water! I've also been a home to important people and during the Second World War, I was occupied by the U.S. Forces Air Raid Precaution! There is nothing more magnificent than to protect and serve!"

"THE WAR?" the weary children asked. "Soldiers are definitely important! Does protecting us during the war make you the most magnificent?"

PETER MINSHALL

BOSCOE HOLDER

SIR V.S. NAIPAUL

DERYCK MURRAY

WENDELL MOTTLEY

"I dare say that education is just as important as the war!" shouted Professor QRC. "I have been educating our nation's children since 1902. Many talented students walked my halls - artists like Peter Minshall, Boscoe Holder and Nobel Prize Winner Sir V.S. Naipaul. Exceptional athletes like cricketer Deryck Murray and Olympic medalist Wendell Mottley trained on my grounds. I've even taught former president George Maxwell Richards and our first Prime Minister, Dr. Eric Williams!"

A.N.R. ROBINSON

GEORGE CHAMBERS

BASDEO PANDAY

DR. ERIC WILLIAMS

"Well that settles it then!" stated Minister Whitehall adamantly. **"I was the headquarters of the U.S. Military during the Second World War! Professor QRC you may have taught the first Prime Minister, but I was chosen for their office!"**

PATRICK MANNING

Shouting erupted as the buildings all started arguing at this suggestion, each boasting, trying to prove their magnificent worth.

Mrs. Mille Fleurs bowed her balcony,

OH DEAR
OH DEAR
WHAT HAVE I DONE!

"Professor QRC, I did not know so many impressive students walked your halls," Mrs. Mille Fleurs whispered.

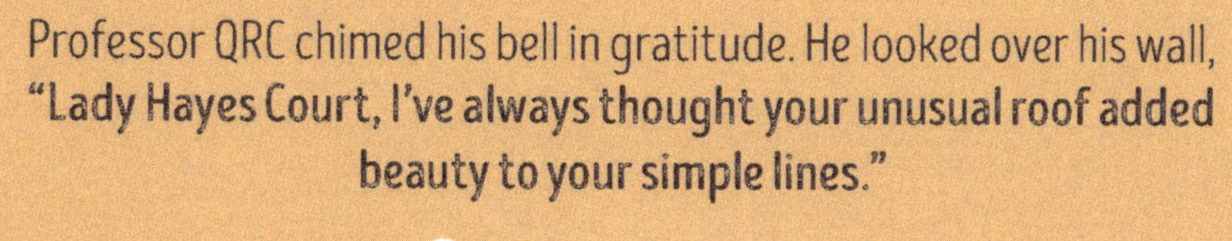

Professor QRC chimed his bell in gratitude. He looked over his wall, **"Lady Hayes Court, I've always thought your unusual roof added beauty to your simple lines."**

THE OTHERS STRUMMED THEIR STEPS IN AGREEMENT!

Lady Hayes Court's railings turned rosy as she blushed. **"Dr. Roomor, your family that built movie theatres, it's amazing that they've lived in you for so many decades!"** she exclaimed.

THE OTHERS BOUNCED THEIR BALCONIES IN AGREEMENT!

Dr. Roomor grinned as she turned to her neighbour, **"It has been my pleasure to be their home. Minister Whitehall, I did not know that you were such a hostess to five Prime Ministers."**

THE OTHERS TAPPED THEIR TILES IN AGREEMENT!

Minister Whitehall curtsied in recognition. She nodded towards The Archbishop, **"Did you really care for Father Bouche? That was so kind of you."**

THE OTHERS SHOOK THEIR SHUTTERS IN AGREEMENT!

The Archbishop raised his arches in appreciation. He said to Sir Stollmeyer, **"None of us might have survived the Second World War if it weren't for you."**

THE OTHERS WINKED THEIR WINDOWS IN AGREEMENT!

Sir Stollmeyer tipped his tower. Finally, to Mrs. Mille Fleurs, he said, **"Well, I didn't know you were a gift from a wife to her husband. That's very romantic."**

Mrs. Mille Fleurs fluttered her fountain at the compliment.

The other houses cheered in agreement
and clapped their doors wildly.

The three children jumped in delight. **"You know children, we've watched the city grow up around us and so much has changed. Sometimes we do feel a bit forgotten."** Mrs. Mille Fleurs looked up and down the street, her glass windows twinkling with pride. **"When you've been around as long as us, you tend to forget the good memories. Thank you so much for helping us to remember the lives that we touched."**

Together all seven houses shouted happily at once

"...And that each of us is

MAGNIFICENT

in our own special way!"